Can you make a necklace
for this lovely lady using
only circles?

This book belongs to:

_____

Here's my favorite
shape:

STERLING CHILDREN'S BOOKS
New York

Can you see a smile?
Color the rest of the grid
to make a portrait!

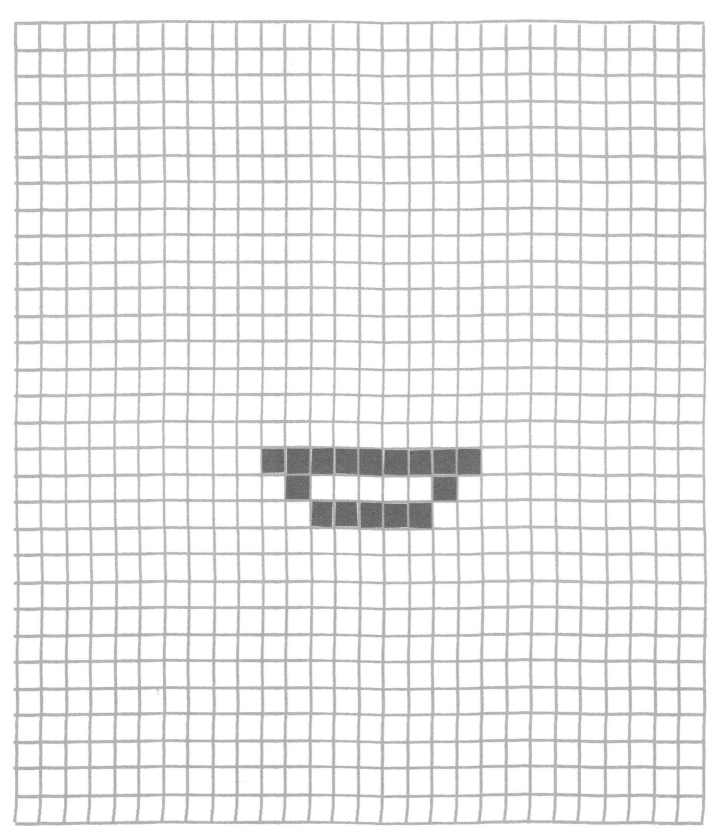

Who is it?

YUM!

See this triangle?
It's a slice of pizza!
Use shapes to create
the topping.
There's already
a piece of pepperoni.

Did you know that a rainbow
is a half of a circle?
Finish this rainbow!

Draw your reflection
using only simple shapes.

Who's going to peek out
of these rectangular windows?

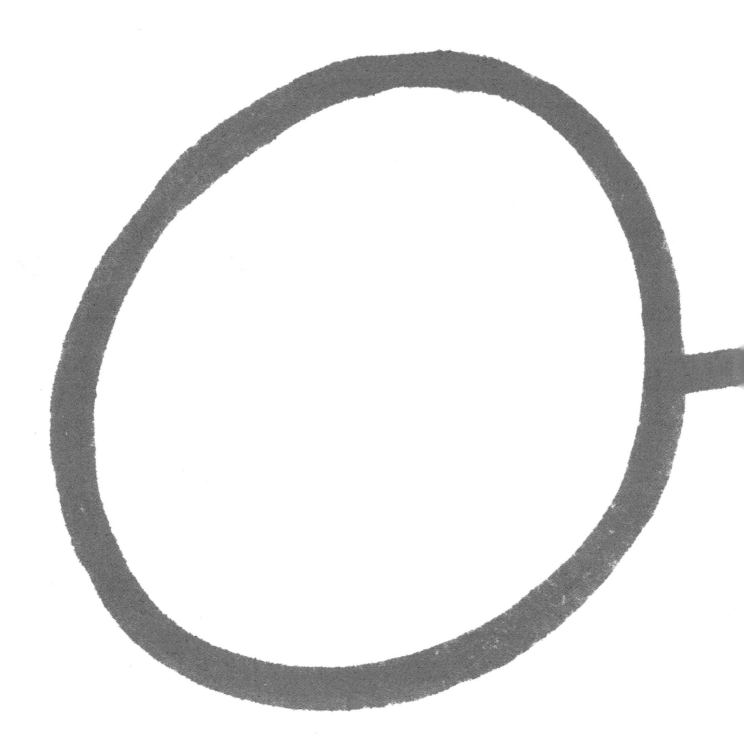

Who's behind these circular glasses?

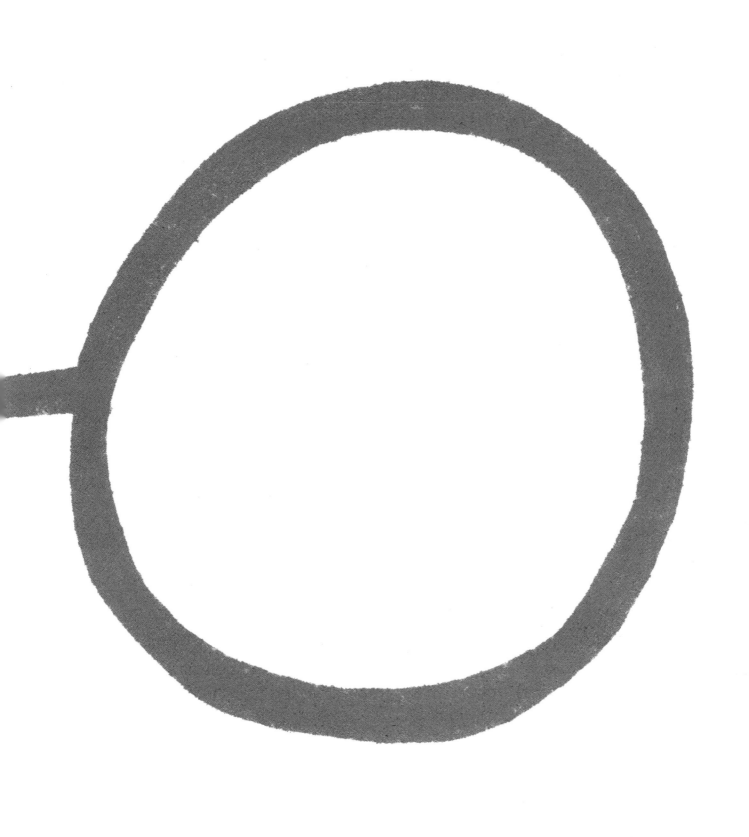

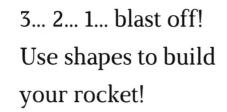

3... 2... 1... blast off!
Use shapes to build
your rocket!

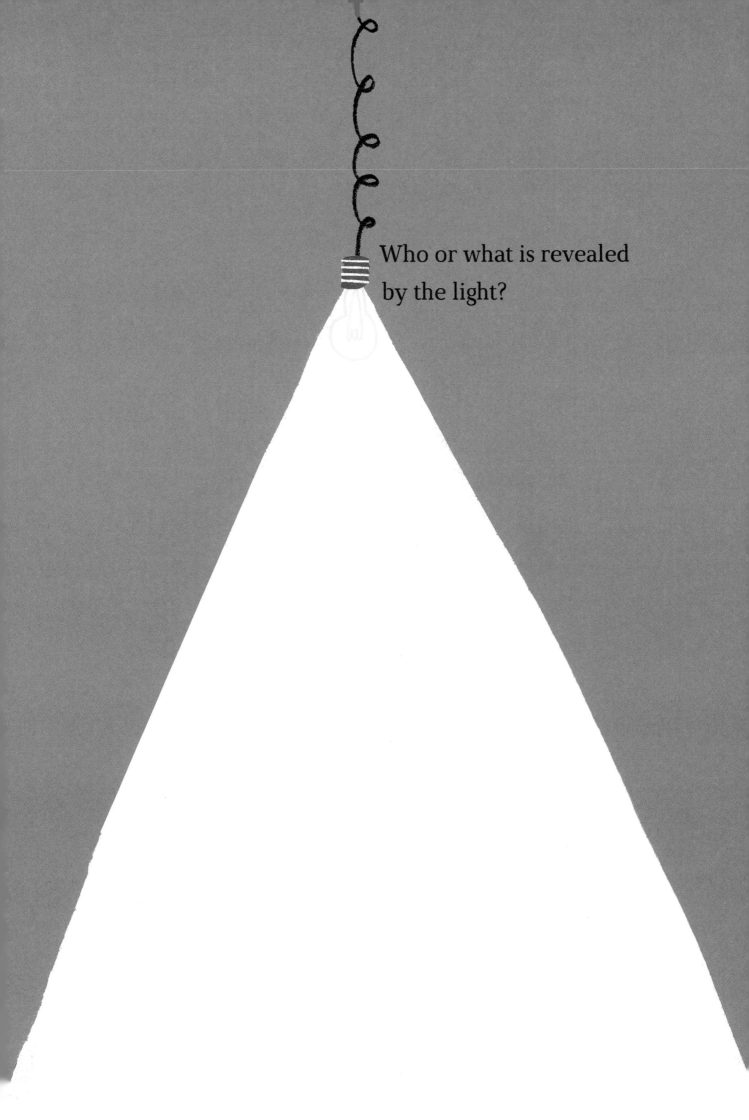

Who or what is revealed by the light?

Fill these rectangles
with pictures for your
newspaper!

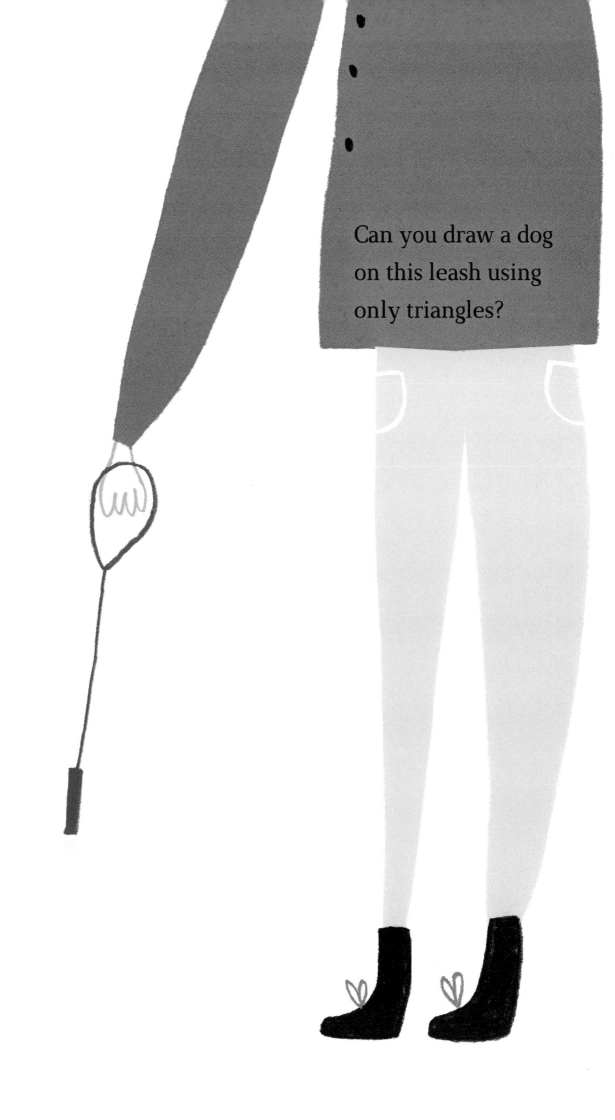

Can you draw a dog
on this leash using
only triangles?

Cut triangles out of paper
and glue them here
to create more icy peaks
and rocky mountains!

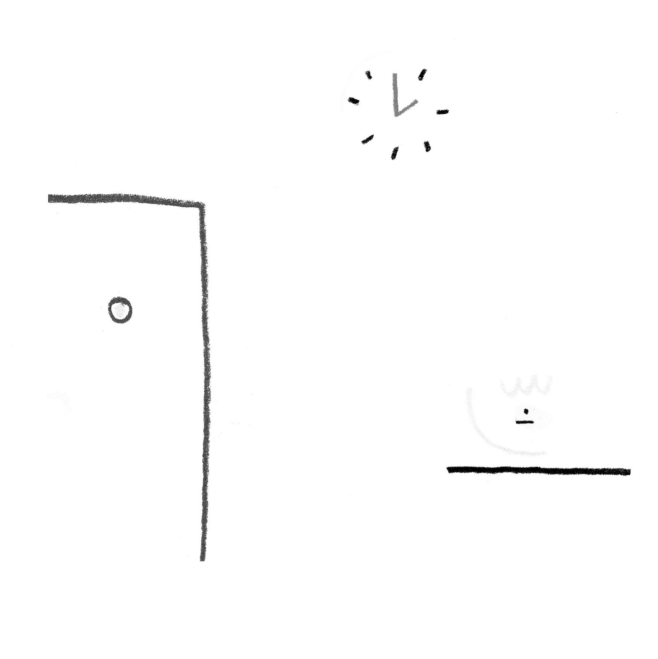

Finish this picture.

Write your name
with letters made
of squares.

Can you make a pretty
pattern for this sweater?
Use just circles
and squares.

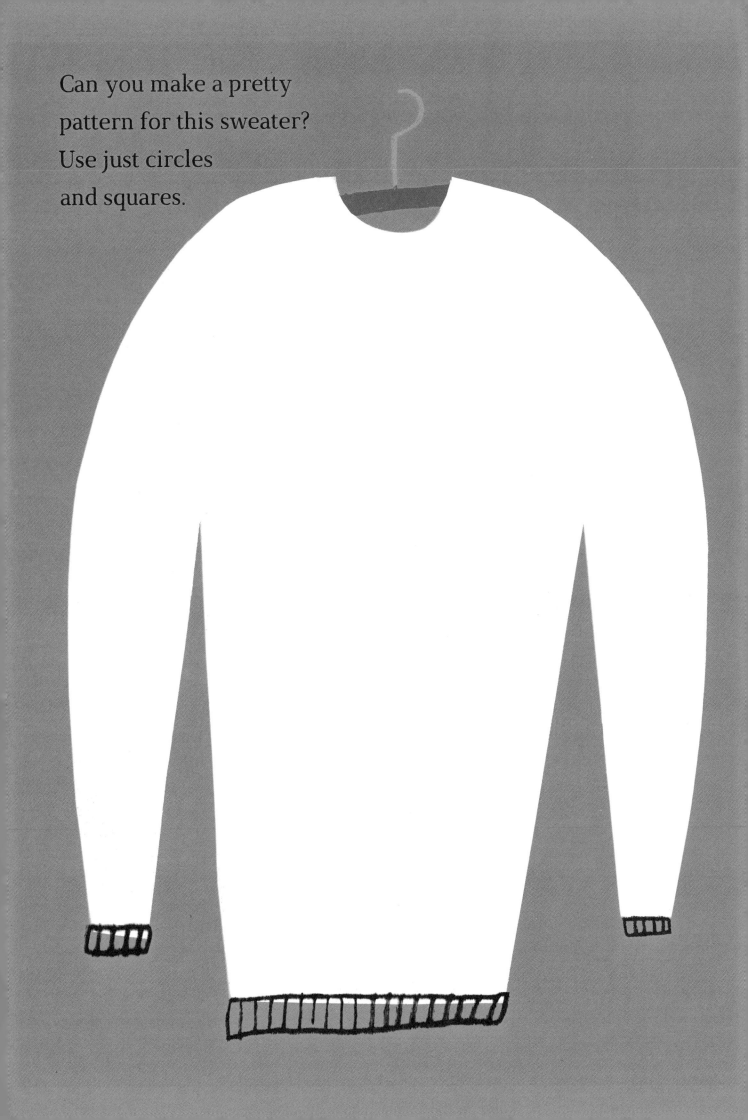

Use simple shapes to make
flower pots and vases.
Then draw some plants
and flowers.

These folks could really use
some hats made with simple shapes.

What can you turn
these shapes into?

Use only circles and draw
as many animals as you
can think of.

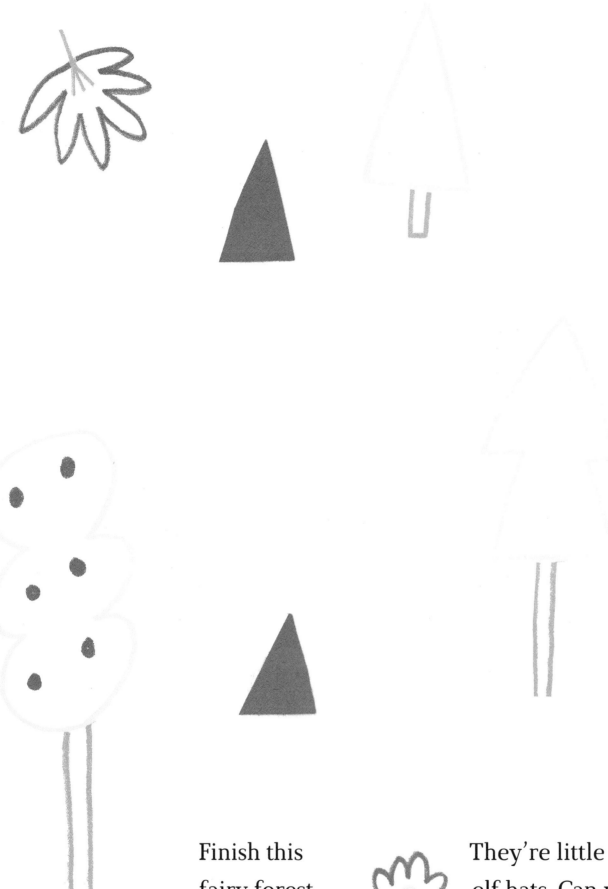

Finish this fairy forest. See those red triangles?

 They're little elf hats. Can you draw the elves underneath them?

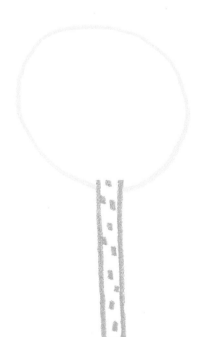

Create a dress
out of circles.

Fill these gift boxes
with toys and candy!

Make a painting using only triangles.

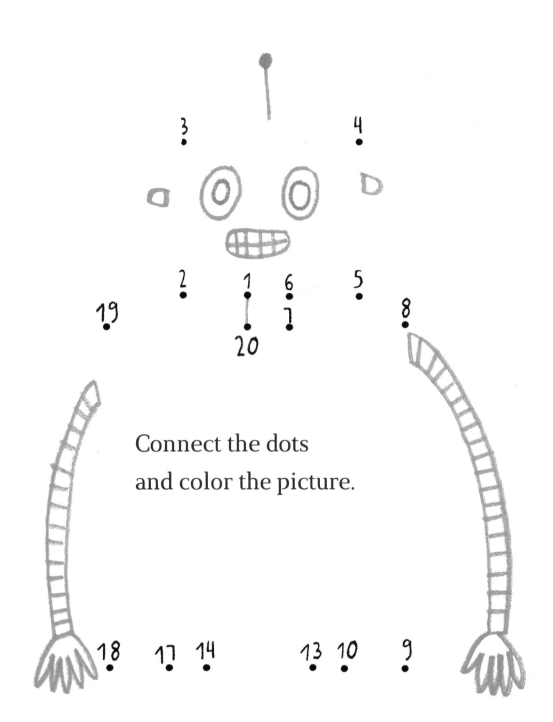

Connect the dots
and color the picture.

Give this athlete
some cool geometric tattoos!

Label these road signs
and draw more
if you want to.

Make a whole picture
out of circles drawn around
a mug or a glass.

Decorate this ancient vase.

What's in the shopping basket?

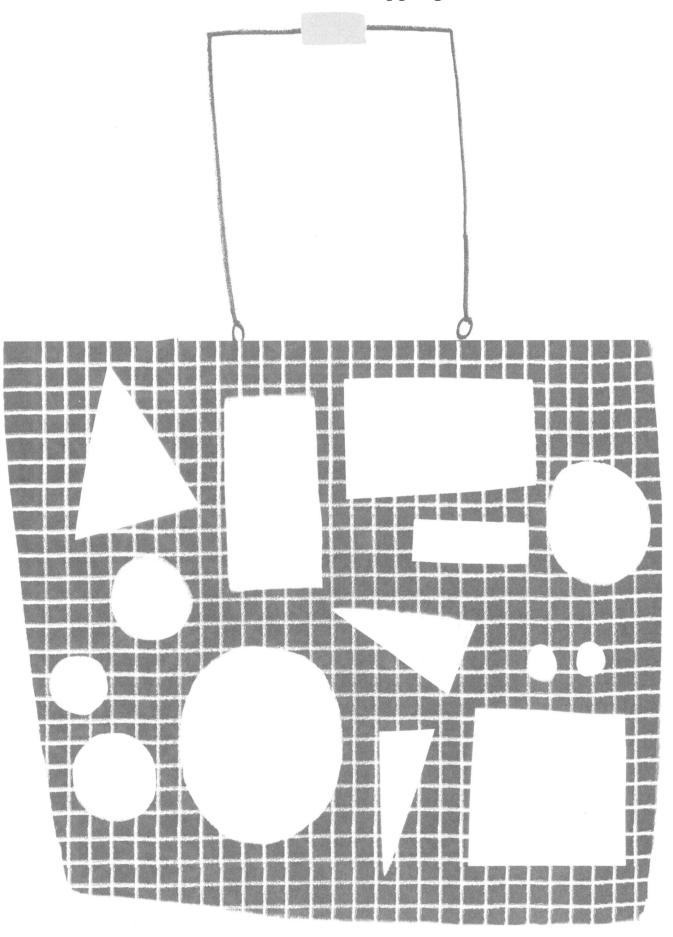

Color the dotted triangles.

Make a sad face and then a happy one!

These triangles are actually
little birds' beaks. Can you draw
the birds to fit them?

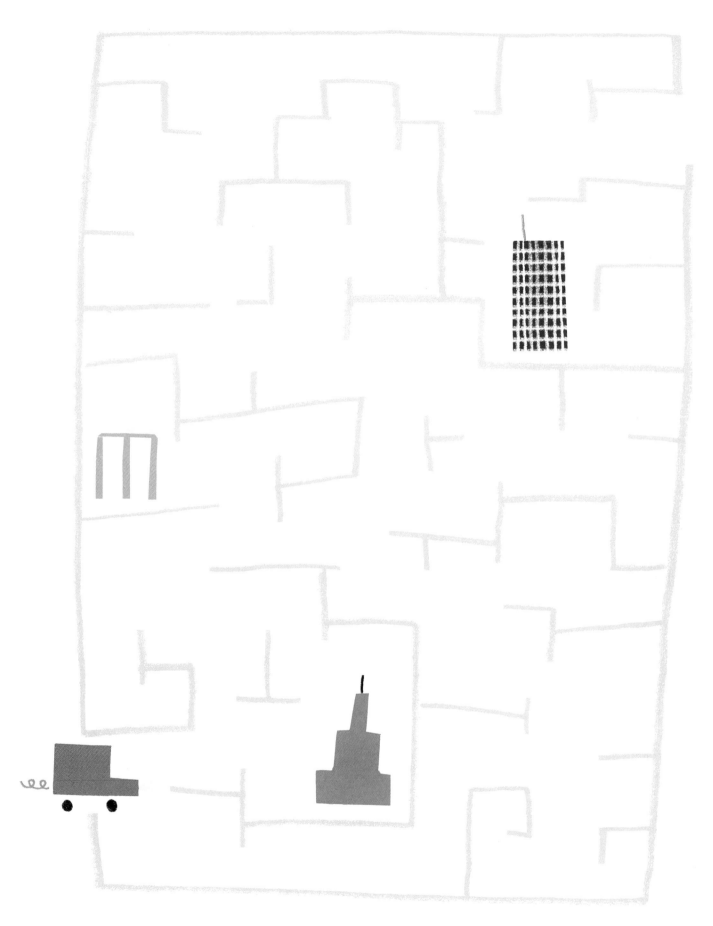

Find this truck's way out of the city.

This red dot could be anything!
Now it's a basketball.
Draw the court and the players.

Finish the castle with simple shapes.

Folding paper into different shapes is called origami.
Make an origami hat!

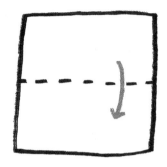

Fold in half.

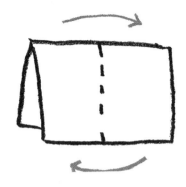

Unfold and fold in
half again in the
other direction.

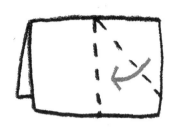

Fold in to
the crease line.

Turn over and repeat
on the other side.

Fold up the bottom
flap and repeat
on the other side.

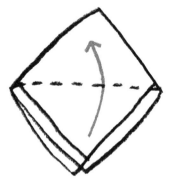

Fold the top part
to the bottom part
and do the same
on the other side.

Awesome!

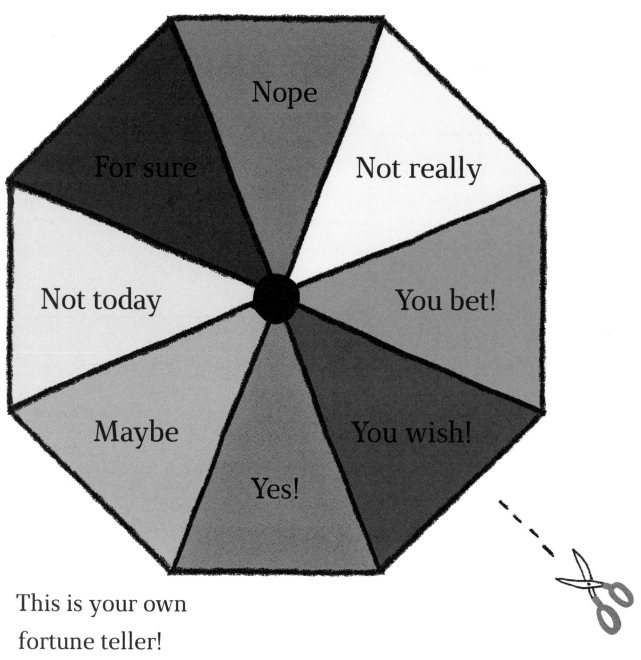

This is your own
fortune teller!
1. Cut it out from this page.
2. Stick a pencil through
   the middle.
3. Ask a question, spin the pencil
   and see where it lands.

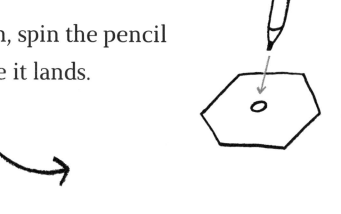

Connect the dots
and color the picture.

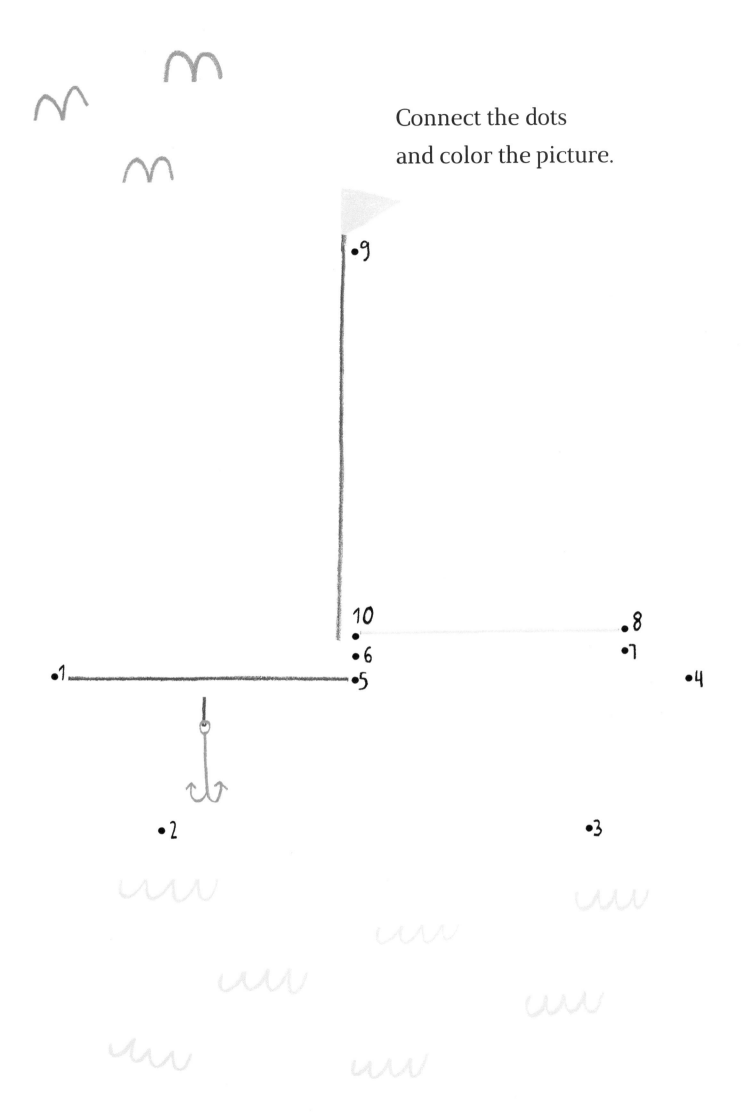

Color the circles and create a picture.
It can be whatever you want. Experiment!

Shapes aren't always simple.

Some shapes are pretty weird.

What could these shapes turn into?

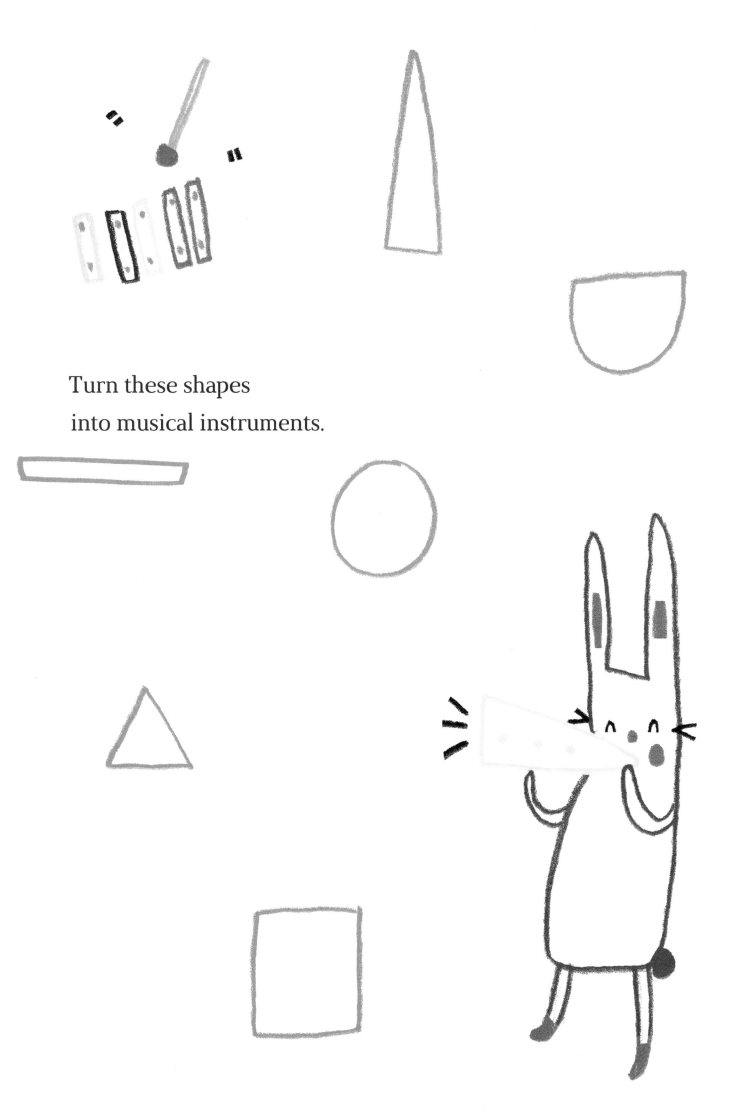

Turn these shapes
into musical instruments.

Hey there, designer!
Draw your own logo
out of squares
and circles.

Cut some rectangles out of black paper and
glue them to this zebra to give it stripes.

This is your window.
Take a peek outside and draw
every triangle you can spot.
A tree, a roof, or maybe
someone's hat?

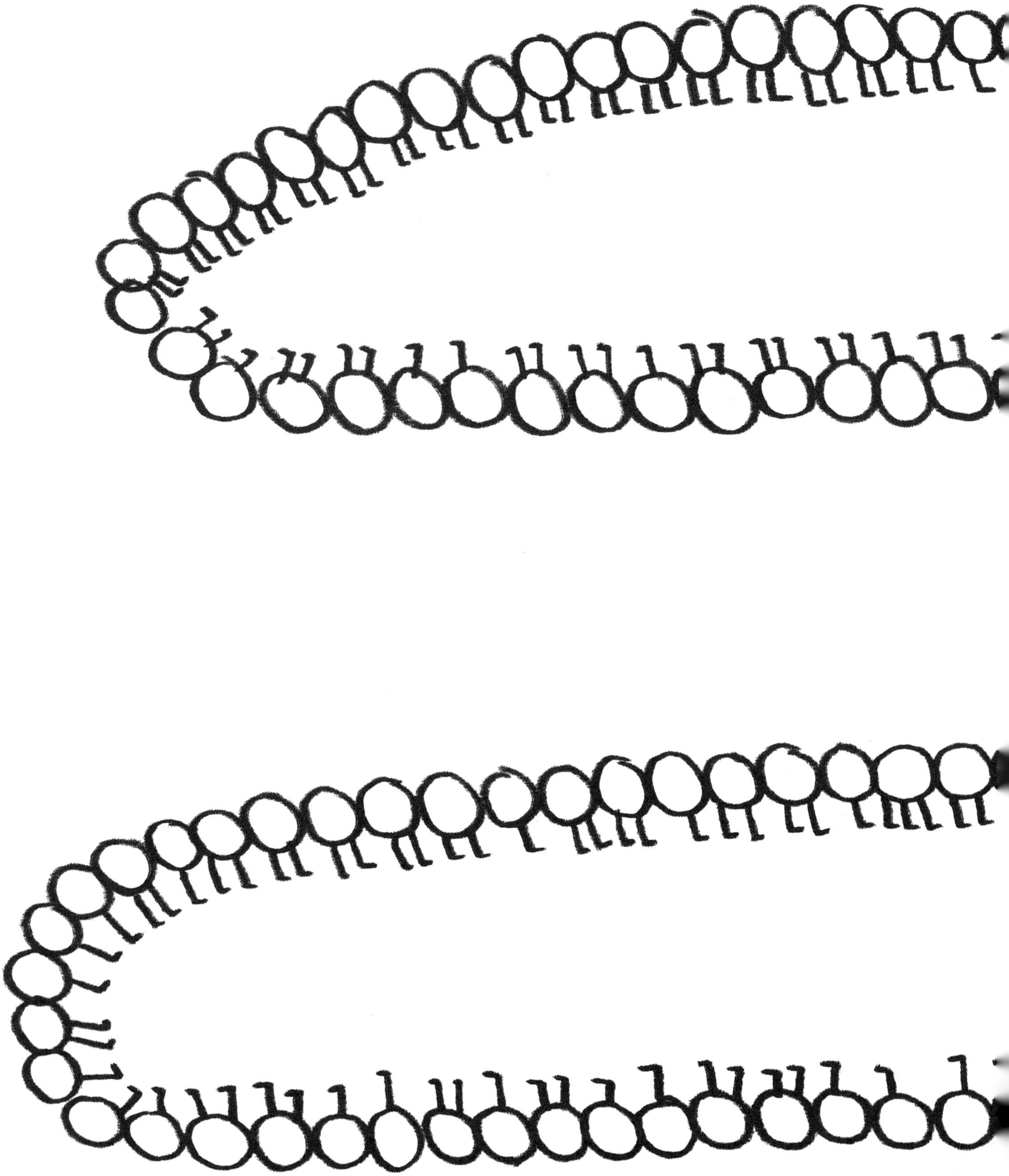

Count how many legs
this little fellow has.
Then color him
with every crayon
you can find!

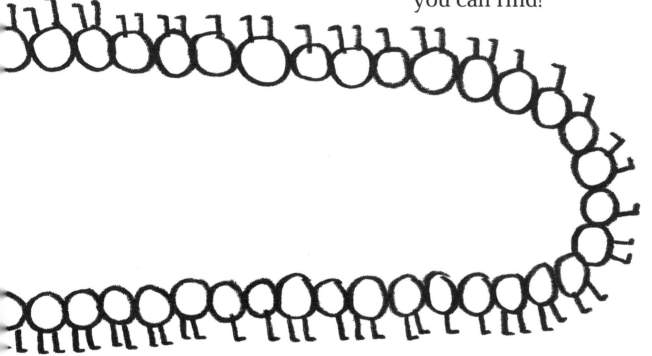

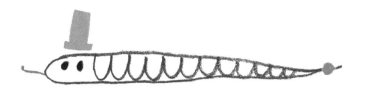

STERLING CHILDREN'S BOOKS
New York

An Imprint of Sterling Publishing
1166 Avenue of the Americas
New York, NY 10036

First Sterling edition published in 2018.

ISBN 978-1-4549-2930-7

Distributed in Canada by Sterling Publishing
c/o Canadian Manda Group, 664 Annette Street -
Toronto, Ontario, M6S 2C8, Canada

For information about custom editions, special sales,
and premium and corporate purchases,
please contact Sterling Special Sales at 800-805-5489
or specialsales@sterlingpublishing.com.

Manufactured in China
Lot #:
2 4 6 8 10 9 7 5 3 1
12/17

sterlingpublishing.com

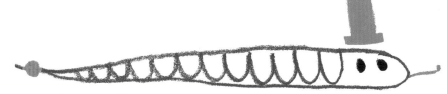

I ♥